D0753176

ALL ABOUT DINOSAURS

TRICERATOPS

by
Amy Allatson

KidHaven
PUBLISHING

PHOTO CREDITS

Abbreviations: l-left, r-right, b-bottom, t-top, c-center, m-middle.

3 – boscorelli. 4-5, 14–15 – Elenarts. 6–9 – robin2. 9bl – boscorellit. 10–12, 16 – Computer Earth. 13 – Catmando. 17tc – Fresnel. 17bc – Linda Bucklin. 18ml – MarcelClemens. 18br – guysal. 18–19background – Iakov Kalinin. 19m – Marques. 20–21 – Catmando.
Images are courtesy of Shutterstock.com, with thanks to Getty Images, Thinkstock Photo, and iStockphoto.

Published in 2018 by
KidHaven Publishing, an Imprint of Greenhaven Publishing, LLC
353 3rd Avenue
Suite 255
New York, NY 10010

Designer: Ian McMullen
Editor: Charlie Ogden

Cataloging-in-Publication Data

Names: Allatson, Amy.
Title: Triceratops / Amy Allatson.
Description: New York : KidHaven Publishing, 2018. | Series: All about dinosaurs | Includes index.
Identifiers: ISBN 9781534521803 (pbk.) | ISBN 9781534521766 (library bound) | ISBN 9781534521681 (6 pack) | ISBN 9781534521728 (ebook)
Subjects: LCSH: Triceratops–Juvenile literature. | Dinosaurs–Juvenile literature.
Classification: LCC QE862.O65 A45 2018 | DDC 567.915'8–dc23

Printed in the United States of America

CPSIA compliance information: Batch #BS17KL: For further information contact Greenhaven Publishing LLC, New York, New York at 1-844-317-7404.

Please visit our website, www.greenhavenpublishing.com. For a free color catalog of all our high-quality books, call toll free 1-844-317-7404 or fax 1-844-317-7405.

CONTENTS

Words that appear like this can be found in the glossary on page 23.

WHAT WERE DINOSAURS?

Dinosaurs were **reptiles** that lived on Earth for more than 160 million years before they became **extinct**.

There were many different types
of dinosaurs. They lived both
on land and in water—and some
could even fly!

WHEN WERE DINOSAURS ALIVE?

Dinosaurs first lived around 230 million years ago during a period of time called the **Mesozoic** Era. The last dinosaurs became extinct around 65 million years ago.

All land on Earth was together in one piece during the time of the dinosaurs. Over time, it has slowly split up into different continents.

EURASIA

NORTH AMERICA

SOUTH AMERICA

AFRICA

ANTARCTICA

PANGEA

WHEN ALL THE LAND ON EARTH WAS TOGETHER IN ONE PIECE, IT WAS CALLED PANGEA.

TRICERATOPS

NAME	Triceratops (try-SEHR-uh-tahps)
LENGTH	30 feet (9 m)
WEIGHT	10 tons (9 mt)
FOOD	herbivore
WHEN IT LIVED	around 65 million years ago
HOW IT MOVED	walked on four legs

Triceratops was a
large dinosaur.

THE NAME *"TRICERATOPS"* MEANS
"THREE-HORNED FACE."

Triceratops became extinct around 65 million years ago. It lived at the same time as *Tyrannosaurus rex* (tuh-RAA-nuh-sohr-uhs REHKS).

TRICERATOPS

WHAT DID TRICERATOPS LOOK LIKE?

Triceratops was around 30 feet (9 m) long and up to 10 feet (3 m) tall. It had a very large head with a bony frill around it.

TRICERATOPS WAS AS HEAVY AS THREE CARS.

Triceratops had three horns on its head. It used these to protect itself against other dinosaurs, such as *Tyrannosaurus rex.*

TYRANNOSAURUS REX

BONY FRILL

HORNS

WHERE DID TRICERATOPS LIVE?

Triceratops lived on land in an area that is now North America. It lived in areas with plenty of **vegetation**.

Some scientists believe *Triceratops* lived in **herds**. They believe this because many *Triceratops* **fossils** have been found together. These dinosaurs might have also traveled together to look for food.

WHAT DID TRICERATOPS EAT?

Triceratops was a herbivore. Its diet was made up of plants, such as ferns and conifers. Its beak-like mouth was useful for grasping plants.

BEAK-LIKE MOUTH

Triceratops was very strong, and many scientists believe that it may have used its three horns to push over large plants.

WAS *TRICERATOPS* THE TOUGHEST DINOSAUR?

Triceratops was one of the toughest dinosaurs to ever live. It had many ways of protecting itself, including its tough skin and strong, sharp horns.

Stegosaurus (steh-guh-SOHR-uhs) was another tough dinosaur. It had armored plates along its back and a spiked tail.

Ankylosaurus (an-kuh-loh-SOHR-uhs) looked similar to an armadillo, except it had spikes down each side of its body.

HOW DO WE KNOW...?

We know so much about dinosaurs thanks to the scientists, called paleontologists, who study them. They dig up fossils of dinosaurs to find out more about them.

FOSSIL

EGG

Scientists put together the bones they find to attempt to make the full skeletons of dinosaurs. From these skeletons, scientists can often figure out the size of a dinosaur. They can also find out information about what it ate from its fossilized food and waste.

SKELETON

SCIENTISTS EVEN FIND FOSSILIZED EGGS AND FOOTPRINTS BELONGING TO DINOSAURS.

FACTS ABOUT TRICERATOPS

A *TRICERATOPS* FOSSIL WAS FOUND WITH BITE MARKS THAT MATCH THOSE OF A *TYRANNOSAURUS REX.*

STRONG LEGS TO SUPPORT ITS HEAVY BODY

30 FEET (9 M)

BONY FRILL

TRICERATOPS HAD ONE OF THE LARGEST SKULLS OF ANY KNOWN DINOSAUR.

TWO LONG HORNS ABOVE THE EYES

NOSE HORN

8-FOOT-LONG (2.4 M) SKULL

BEAK-LIKE MOUTH

DRAW YOUR OWN DINOSAUR

THINK ABOUT THESE QUESTIONS...

1. How does it move?
2. Does it live on land or in water?
3. What does it eat?
4. What color is it?
5. How big is it?

GLOSSARY

armored covered in a protective layer

continents any of the seven great masses of land on Earth

extinct no longer alive

fossils the remains of plants and animals that lived a long time ago

herbivore a plant-eating animal

herds groups of animals that live together

Mesozoic a period of time when dinosaurs lived from 252.2 million years ago to 66 million years ago

reptiles cold-blooded animals with scales

vegetation plants found in a particular area

INDEX